LATIN
FOR EVEN MORE
OCCASIONS

Lingua Latina
Multo Pluribus Occasionibus

LINGUA LATINA MULTO PLURIBUS OCCASIONIBUS

HENRICUS BARBATUS
SCRIPSIT

Liber Joannis Narratoris
Conlegarumque

LIBRI VILLARDI NOVI EBORACI
A.U.C. MMDCCXLIV

LATIN
FOR
EVEN MORE
OCCASIONS

BY
HENRY BEARD

A John Boswell Associates Book

VILLARD BOOKS NEW YORK
A.D. MCMXCI

Library of Congress Cataloging-in-Publication Data

Beard, Henry.
Latin for even more occasions / by Henry Beard =
Lingua Latina multo pluribus occasionibus /
Henricus Barbatus Scripsit.—1st ed.
p.   cm.
"A John Boswell Associates book."
ISBN 0-679-40674-3
1. Latin language—Conversation and phrase books—English.
2. Latin language—Humor.   I. Title.   II. Title: Lingua Latina
multo pluribus occasionibus.
PA2107.B39   1991   478.3'421—dc20   91-22495

Manufactured in the United States of America
3 5 7 9 8 6 4 2

This book was set in 9/12 Linotron Trump Medieval.

Book design by Carole Lowenstein

Oh, darn, there I go again! You know, I just can't help speaking Latin.

Ecce, denuo ago, sicut soleo! Non enim possum facere quin Latine loquar.

It's so second nature to me, sometimes I don't even know I'm doing it!

Adeo huius mihi rei natura facta est, ut interdum nesciam quidem me sic facere!

PREFACE
Praefatio

As you can tell from the title of this book, *Lingua Latina Multo Pluribus Occasionibus* (Latin for Even More Occasions) is a sequel. It was written as a companion volume to *Lingua Latina Occasionibus Omnibus* (Latin for All Occasions), but it is also a complete work in its own right, containing hundreds of all-new translations of everyday English expressions into grammatically accurate, idiomatically correct classical Latin, and incorporating the same foolproof, easy-to-use Latin pronunciation guide found in its predecessor.

Now, even though the word "sequel" comes directly from Latin (you probably spotted it right away as a derivative of the third-conjugation deponent verb *sequor, sequi, secutus sum*: to follow) and even though the *Aeneid*, Virgil's precedent-setting epic poem, has *twelve* books, the fact is, we never planned to produce a follow-up to our original collection of handy conversational Latin phrases.

Frankly, the reason why we chose a sweeping title like *Lingua Latina Occasionibus Omnibus* (Latin for All Occasions) in the first place, instead of something safer like *Iam Ardebat Cum Citheram Meam Sustuli* (It Was On Fire When I Picked Up My Fiddle) was that we truly felt that the book had not only thoroughly covered the territory in question, but had looted it, subjugated it, and built a pretty impressive system of roads and aqueducts across it.

Well, *peccavimus* (we goofed). Even though our *magnum opus* (magnum opus) included everything from cocktail-party chitchat and singles-bar banter to high-powered business buzzwords and Hollywood mogul jargon, the many letters we've received since its publication from readers seeking the precise translation of a phrase that wasn't in the book but was right on the tips of their tongues (in some cases, the lines in question occupied their entire tongue surfaces) soon convinced us that more work remained to be done.

How, they wanted to know, do you say "Please don't squeeze the Charmin"? Should it have the polite *Noli* and an infinitive, or the poetic *Ne* and an imperative? When you croon "You Can't Always Get What You Want" in the shower, do you have to vocalize in the subjunctive? Can you say "I'm a rambling wreck from Georgia Tech" without using a gerund?

We also had numerous requests from people who needed a little assistance with Latin composition for specific purposes we hadn't thought of: like a brief after-dinner speech in the language of Cicero for those annoying occasions when some complete *podex* (aggravating person) calls upon you to make a few impromptu remarks; or a two-minute comedy routine worthy of Plautus so you can use a dead language to become the life of the party; or a bit of light-hearted infield chatter from the Campus Martius to unnerve the opposition in a friendly softball game.

Needless to say, we quickly realized that we had not only the opportunity, but also the obligation, to produce a second compendium of impeccably accurate Roman chin music to help those many classically trained individuals whose Latin is just a little rusty to "chew the toga" with absolute confidence. And of course it was that very real sense of duty, and not some cynical desire to "*lucrifacere*" ("cash in") on an improbable fad that we inadvertently created, that led to *Lingua Latina Multo Pluribus Occasionibus* (Latin for Even More Occasions).

At this point, some *mentula* (difficult individual) might be tempted to ask, "So, is this series going to have a third part someday?"

Really. Of all the Gaul.

Salvete ('Bye) and *Die dulci fruimini* (Have a nice day)!

ACKNOWLEDGMENTS
Gratiae

I would like to thank Mark Sugars, who not only corrected the many inflectional errors and grammatical inaccuracies in my manuscript but also suggested countless changes, both large and small, which have conferred on this book a degree of classical polish and linguistic refinement that I could never have produced on my own. If there are any laurels handed out for a particularly well chosen phrase or elegant piece of diction, his brow is the appropriate repository for the honorary vegetation. If, on the other hand, there are any howlingly infelicitous constructions or outright boo-boos, the dunce cap belongs on my noggin.

I would also like to note for the record, now that the success of *Lingua Latina Occasionibus Omnibus* (Latin for All Occasions) makes it clear that I am engaging in a sincere effort to share the credit rather than a transparent attempt to shift the blame, that the idea for these books was entirely John Boswell's, as was the overall concept for their format. And I'd also like to express our gratitude to Peter Gethers, whose bold (some might say foolhardy) decision to publish a collection of conversational Latin phrases makes Hannibal's crossing of the Alps by elephant seem by comparison a pretty ho-hum pachyderm deployment.

H.B.

CONTENTS
Quod in Libro Continetur

FRENCH SOUNDS EVEN BETTER IN LATIN

Savoir faire
- *Scire facere*

Déjà vu
- *Prius visum*

Nouveau riche
- *Novissime locupletatus*

Joie de vivre
- *Gaudium vivendi*

De rigueur
- *Coactus*

Tête-à-tête
- *Capitibus conlatis*

Comme ci, comme ça
- *Medio, modico*

Plus ça change, plus c'est la même chose
- *Quo magis mutat, eo magis perstat*

Merde!
- *Merda!*

LATIN: IT'S MORE THAN A LANGUAGE—IT'S AN ATTITUDE

Yes, I have a personal Latin trainer.
- *Aio, exercitorem linguae Latinae proprium habeo.*

We're working on my ablatives and subjunctives.
- *Exercemus casus ablativos et modos subjunctivos meos.*

I want to get my syntax into shape for the beach this summer.
- *Volo ut syntaxis mea splendescat in litore, veniente aestate.*

THE BASIC PHILOSOPHIES ARE BEST EXPRESSED IN LATIN

I think, therefore I am.
- *Cogito, ergo sum.*

I am, therefore I eat.
- *Sum, ergo edo.*

I think, therefore I am depressed.
- *Cogito, ergo doleo.*

I think I'll have another drink.
- *Cogito sumere potum alterum.*

ALL BOOKS ARE GREAT BOOKS IN LATIN

Glitter
- *Fulgor*

Princess Daisy
- *Regis Filia Composita*

Valley of the Dolls
- *Valles Puparum*

Once Is Not Enough
- *Semel Non Satis Est*

Smart Women, Foolish Choices
- *Mulieres Sapientes, Optiones Ineptae*

Living, Loving, and Learning
- *Vivere, Amare, Discere*

I'm OK—You're OK
- *Valeo—Vales*

Everything You Always Wanted to Know About Sex but Were Afraid to Ask
- *Omnia Quae De Sexu Cognoscere Semper Voluisti sed Rogare Metuisti*

SNIPPETS OF POETRY ARE EASIER TO WEDGE INTO THE CONVERSATION IN LATIN

A rose is a rose is a rose.
- *Rosa rosa rosa est est.*

Do I dare to eat a peach?
- *Audeone persicum edere?*

Not with a bang but a whimper
- *Non crepitu, sed vagitu*

And quoth the Raven, "Nevermore!"
- *Ac dixit Corvus, "Numquam postea!"*

DOPEY EXHORTATIONS ARE MORE FORCEFUL IN LATIN

Go with the flow.
- *Ventis secundis, tene cursum.*

Don't let the bastards wear you down.
- *Noli nothis permittere te terere.*

Lead, follow, or get out of the way.
- *Duc, sequere, aut de via decede.*

Let it all hang out.
- *Totum dependeat.*

THERE IS NO SUCH THING AS A STUPID QUESTION IN LATIN

What, in a nutshell, is deconstructionism?
- *Paucis verbis, quid est deconstructionismus?*

Who exactly are the Kurds?
- *Quinam sunt Carduchi?*

Wouldn't nuclear winter cancel out the greenhouse effect?
- *Nonne hiems, quae incendiis magnis multisque belli inter gentes omnes tertii inducatur, inhibeat orbem terrarum ne nimium calescat?*

If you put a little pyramid on top, does that make something postmodern?
- *Si in culmine pyramidem parvam superponas, ita fit postnovitas?*

Your Two Cents' Worth Goes a Lot Farther in Latin

I'd much rather have a '55 Thunderbird than a '58 Corvette.
- *Magnopere malim Tonitravem anni MCMLV quam Corvettam anni MCMLVIII.*

Ali could have beaten Tyson.
- *Ali Tysonem vicisset, si pugnavissent.*

You really shouldn't keep a dog in the city.
- *Canis in urbe custodiendus non est.*

All frozen pizzas taste lousy.
- *Omnes lagani pistrinae gelati male sapiunt.*

You can't get a decent sound system for under a grand.
- *Non potes composituram machinarum quae apte musicam faciunt emere minoris quam mille.*

THINGS TO SAY TO THE MAÎTRE D' WHEN YOU DON'T HAVE A RESERVATION

Could you check again? My name must be there.
- *Inspice, sodes, denuo. Certo scio nomen adesse.*

I don't understand. My secretary called a week ago.
- *Non intellego. Scriba mea tibi filo dixit septem diebus ante.*

Listen, I have a very important business client with me.
- *Audi, mecum habeo socium in negotiis magni momenti.*

He's also my oldest friend.
- *Insuper etiam est amicus veterrimus.*

It's both of our birthdays.
- *Haec est nobis ambobus dies natalis.*

I'm a restaurant reviewer.
- *Cauponas percenseo.*

Here's ten bucks.
- *Ecce, tibi do decem denarium.*

Pretty please with cherry on top!
- *Te precor dulcissime supplex!*

LAS VEGAS LATIN

Are these slots progressive?
• *Crescuntne gradatim praedae ab his latronibus unibrachiis?*

I hit the jackpot!
• *Copiam cepi!*

Come on, baby needs a new pair of shoes!
• *Age, infanti opus est pari novorum calceorum!*

Damn! Snake eyes!
• *Vae! Canes!*

A fresh deck please, and cut 'em thin to win!
• *Sis, fer sarcinam recentem chartularum, et parti illas impariter ut praedas paremus!*

LATIN FOR THE LOTTERY

Do you have any tickets with Roman numerals?
• *Habesne ullas tesseras numeris Romanis impressas?*

No wonder I never win!
• *Non miror me numquam vicisse!*

II.
PERSONAL LATIN
Lingua Latina Propria

LATIN: THE PERFECT PREPPY PATOIS

Let's mix up a pitcher of Bloodys, get crocked, and drop trou!
- *In urceo numerum Sanguineorum misceamus, ebrii fiamus, et bracas demittamus!*

Excellent! Intense quaffing action!
- *Praestantem! Nunc est adsiduo perpotandum!*

Major party bore! Biff's going to toss his tacos!
- *Taedium convivii maius! Byphis vomiturus est!*

He has to drive the big white bus to Woof City!
- *Sibi necesse est agere magnam raedam albam ad Municipium Eiectamenti!*

Let's bolt!
- *Evolemus!*

We're golden!
- *Aurei sumus!*

Aurelian Wall Street Latin

Greed is good.
- *Avaritia bona est.*

The name of the game is leverage.
- *Lusus cum pecunia mutua sumpta tibi ludendus est.*

I am a Master of the Universe!
- *Magister Mundi sum!*

I'm taking the Fifth!
- *Cito Emendationem Quintam!*

Latin: The Ultimate Yuppie Lingo

My Rolex is waterproof to twelve hundred meters.
- *Rolex meum vim aquae potest resistere usque ad altitudinem trium milium septingentorum pedum.*

I have a fax machine in my BMW.
- *In curro meo ab Officina Baiuoaria Mechanica fabricato habeo machinam quae litteras per aethera transmittit.*

I know a restaurant with only one table.
- *Novi cauponam quae solum unam mensam habet.*

My jogging suit is by Armani.
- *Armanius tunicam meam, quae apta est currendo, fecit.*

My Jacuzzi is filled with Perrier.
- *Meum balineum calidum verticosum cum aqua scintillante fontana Gallica impletum est.*

My bankruptcy lawyer is Alan Dershowitz.
- *Ego decoctor iuris consulto Alano Dershowitzi utor.*

HACKER LATIN: THE USER-FRIENDLY COMPUTER LANGUAGE

How's hacking, chiphead?
* *Quid agis, caput assulae?*

My motherboard fried! I am in a pessimal mode!
* *Tabula materna combusta est! Sum in modo pessimo!*

Some bagbiting technoweenie put a hungus Trojan horse in my program! It is munged!
* *Artifex plumipes qui merdam manducat in meo libello electronico qui regit computatorem equum Troianum posuit! Pessum datum est!*

I am globally torqued! Moby bogosity!
* *Funditus tortus sum! Fucatissimum!*

GOLDEN-AGE LATIN FOR NEW-AGE PEOPLE

Pyramids are out. I'm putting all my crystals in a little domed box shaped like the Pantheon.
- *Pyramides obsoletae sunt. Servo omnes gemmas crystallinas meas in cista formata in tholum instar Pantheonis.*

Using the subjunctive generates more alpha waves than meditation.
- *Modus subiunctivus gignit plus fluctuum alpha quam meditatio.*

Obviously your id, ego, and libido are going to be able to express themselves more fully in their native language—Latin.
- *Manifesto id, ego, et libido poterunt plenius se declarare lingua indigena—Latina videlicet.*

Roman numerology is a thousand years older than any Johnny-come-lately systems based on Arabic squiggles.
- *Vaticinatio quae numeris Romanis utitur vetustior est milibus annis quam ulla ratio sera quae scriptis Arabicis utitur.*

Om!
- *Omo, omas, omat, omamus, omatus, omant!*

LATIN IS ALWAYS POLITICALLY CORRECT

I sing of arms and a dead white male.
- *Arma virumque flavum atque mortuum cano.*

I came, I saw, I spoke out on a number of critical Third World issues.
- *Veni, vidi, verba feci de pluribus gravibus pertinentibus ad Partem Tertiam Orbis Terrarum, quae, ut scis, in partes tres divisa est.*

Languages that don't have separate genders are sexist!
- *Linguae quae genera distincta non habent inuriam faciunt feminis!*

Let us firmly reject all commands, conditions, and prohibitions that are not expressed in the subjunctive!
- *Repudiemus obstinate omnia mandata et condiciones et interdicta quae in modo subiunctivo non expressa sint!*

TIBER VALLEY GIRL

I'm, you know, in the mall, and I'm like talking to this major
 studmuffin?
- *Sum enim in foro, et modo, en, loquor cum quodam Adonide
 mero?*

It was totally awesome—I mean, really copious rad!
- *Omnino mirabile fuit—volo dicere, vero probe r. licitus!*

And then I had negative clues, and I misused the subjunctive.
- *Tum autem indicia mihi erant obscura, et modo subiunctivo
 abusa sum.*

What a buzzstomp! Multiple sadness! I was mega raked!
- *O stridorem conculcatorum! Maestiam multiplicatam! Magnopere excruciata sum!*

Gag me with a spoon!
- *Fac me cocleario vomere!*

Funny, You Don't Look Latinish

Oy vay, what a—
• *Eheu, qualem—*

> klutz!
> *inhabilem!*

> schnook!
> *blennum!*

> schlemiel!
> *virum laevum!*

> yenta!
> *oblatratricem!*

> gonif!
> *furem!*

> schnorrer!
> *parasitum!*

> kibitzer!
> *interpellatorem!*

> nebbish!
> *tenuiculum!*

> putz!
> *verpam!*

> momser!
> *nothum!*

> schmuck!
> *mentulam!*

CHARIOTS OF THE ROMANS?

Okay, so if Plautus didn't write Shakespeare's plays, how come so many of them are set in Italy?
- *Ne scripserit Plautus Shakespearii fabulas, quamobrem tot actae sunt utentes scaena Italica!*

Did you ever ask yourself why all the craters on the moon have *Latin* names?
- *Rogavistine umquam te ipsum cur sint omnibus crateribus in luna nomina* Latina!

Atlantis—Atlantic City. Think about it.
- *Atlantis—Urbs Atlantica. Cogita de hoc.*

III.
CONVIVIAL LATIN
Lingua Latina Hilaris

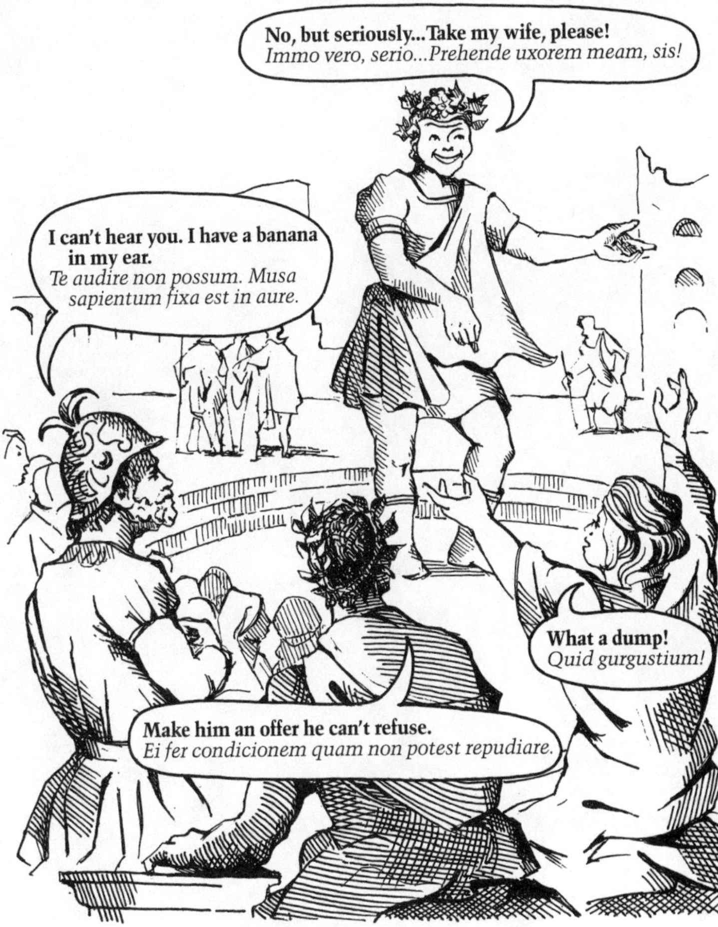

Punch Lines Have More Punch in Latin

I can't hear you. I have a banana in my ear.
- *Te audire non possum. Musa sapientum fixa est in aure.*

You know, that dog isn't really all *that* shaggy.
- *Re vera, canis ille nequaquam* adeo *pilosus est.*

And at these prices, you won't see many more kangaroos in this bar, either.
- *Et tantis pretiis constitutis plures Macropodidas in hac caupona minime videbis.*

Wisecracks Are Wiser in Latin

Is that a scroll in your toga, or are you just happy to see me?
- *Estne volumen in toga, an solum tibi libet me videre?*

Take a picture, it lasts longer!
- *Fac imaginem, diutius durabit!*

Anyone Can Do a Great Impression—in Latin

JAMES CAGNEY
You dirty rat!
- *Tu, rattus turpis!*

MARLON BRANDO
I could've been a contender.
- *Proeliator fuissem.*

Make him an offer he can't refuse.
- *Ei fer condicionem quam non potest repudiare.*

CLINT EASTWOOD
Go ahead. Make my day.
- *Age. Fac ut gaudeam.*

CARY GRANT
Judy, Judy, Judy.
- *Iudaea, Iudaea, Iudaea.*

W. C. FIELDS
It was a woman who drove me to drink. I never stopped to
thank her.
- *Fuit mulier quae me potare egit. Nunquam steti gradum ad ei gratias agendas.*

GROUCHO
I like my cigar, too, but I take it out of my mouth once in
a while.
- *Fasciculum nicotianum fumificum meum quoque amo, sed aliquando eum de ore extraho.*

MAE WEST

Come up and see me sometime.

- *Interdum ascende ut me visas.*

LAUREN BACALL

You know how to whistle, don't you? Just put your lips
   together and blow.

- *Nonne scis sibilare! Labris compositis, perfla.*

BETTE DAVIS

What a dump!

- *Quid gurgustium!*

COMEDY NIGHT AT CAESAR'S PALACE

Take my wife, please!
- *Prehende uxorem meam, sis!*

No, but seriously . . .
- *Immo vero, serio . . .*

I just flew in from Gaul—boy, are my arms tired!
- *Nuperrime de Gallia huc volavi—Mehercle, bracchia mea defatigata sunt!*

Anyone here from Rome?
- *Adestne quisquam de Roma?*

Listen: I just got the latest score from the Colosseum—Lions 32, Christians 0, in sudden-death overtime!
- *Audite: Modo de Colosseo rationem interfectorum recentissimam cognovi—Leonibus triginta duo, Christianis nihil, clepsydra addita ad spatium mortis subitae!*

Do you know how many barbarians it takes to light a torch? One million—one to hold the torch, and the rest to get together and try to discover fire!
- *Scitisne quantus numerus barbarorum satis est ut ipsi facem accendere possint? Decies centena milia—uno facem tenente, debent ceteri convenire atque conari ignem invenire!*

You're just like my agent—you get ten percent of my jokes!
- *Simillimi procuratoris mei estis—iocorum meorum partem decimam prehenditis!*

But really, you've been a beautiful audience! I love ya, I love ya!
- *Sed vere, spectatores pulchri fuistis! Vos amo! Vos amo!*

A SIDESPLITTING LATIN TELEPHONE ANSWERING-MACHINE PRANK

FIRST CALL:

This is the Vatican calling for the pope. We need a ruling on a venial sin.

- *Hoc est Vaticanum. Pontificem maximum filo vocamus. Nobis opus est arbitrio de peccato veniale.*

SECOND CALL:

This is the College of Cardinals calling for the pope. We hope you can make it to the tailgate party next Saturday.

- *Hoc est Conlegium Cardinalium pontificem maximum filo vocans. Speramus te venturus esse ad convivium in tergis raedarum die Saturni proxima.*

THIRD CALL:

This is the caretaker at Castel Gondolfo. Your Holiness, do you want me to prune these olive trees?

- *Hic est custos Castelli Gondolfi. Papa Sanctissime, visne ut illas oleas putem!*

FOURTH CALL:

Hi, this is the pope. Have there been any messages for me?

- *Ave, hic est pontifex maximus qui tibi filo dicit. Mihine nuntia ulla fuerunt!*

A LATIN TONGUE TWISTER

How much wood would a woodchuck chuck if a woodchuck
    could chuck wood?
- *Quantum materiae materietur marmota monax si marmota
  monax materiam possit materiari?*

Just as much wood as a woodchuck would if a woodchuck
    could chuck wood.
- *Tantum materiae quam materietur marmota monax si marmota
  monax materiam possit materiari.*

THINGS TO SAY AT A TOGA PARTY

Are you wearing anything under that sheet?
- *Ullamne subuculam geris?*

Toga! Toga! Toga!
- *Togam! Togam! Togam!*

AN ALL-PURPOSE WEDDING TOAST

I'd like to propose a toast to the happy couple and their
    incompatability: His *income,* and her *pat-ability*!
- *Ego coniugibus felicibus propino: Scin quam inter se diversitas
  sit? Is dives, ea versuta est!*

AN ALL-PURPOSE LATIN AFTER-DINNER SPEECH

You all probably think I am going to say something weighty
and memorable in Latin. Well, I'm not. What I'm going
to do is read you my laundry list. Here it is. Three pairs
of socks, five underwear, two shirts, no starch. There,
that's it. You can applaud now. Have a nice day.

- *Vos omnes fortasse creditis me aliquid grave ac memorabile
Latine dicturum esse. Re vera, illud facere non in animo habeo. Etenim perlecturus sum vobis catalogum lavandariorum.
Hic incipit. Tibialium paria tria, subuncularum quinque, tun-
icae duae, nullum amylum. Sic, actum est. Mihi plaudere nunc
potestis. Die dulci fruimini.*

IV.
REGIONAL LATIN
Lingua Latina Domi

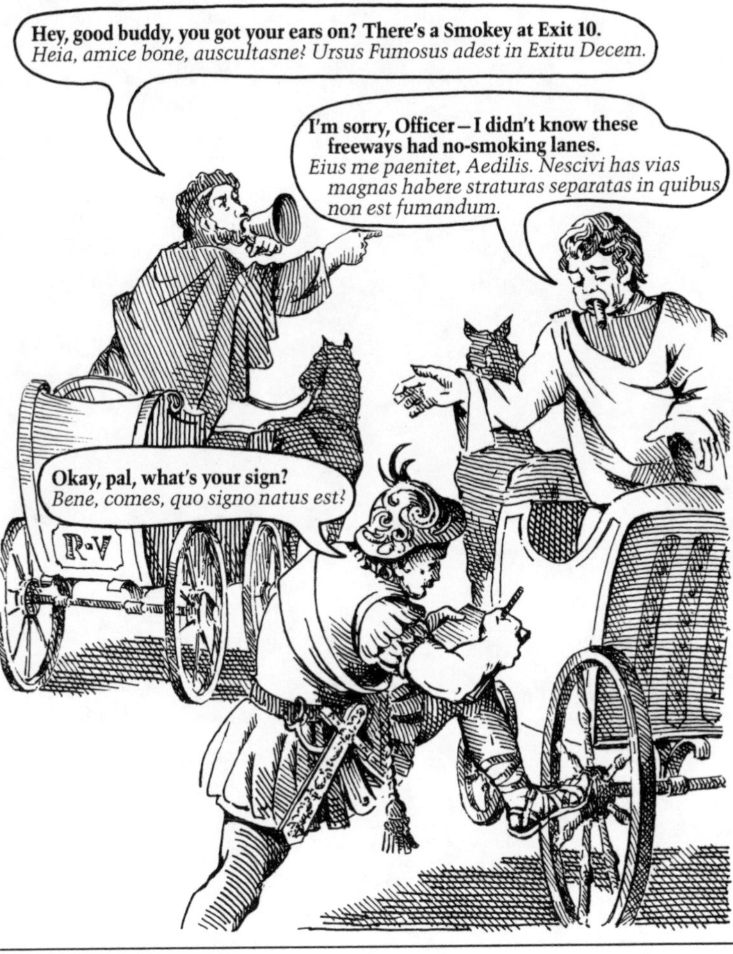

With Latin, All Roads Lead to Your Hometown

Beantown
Urbs Fabarum

The Big Apple
Malum Magnum

The Big Easy
Facilitas Magna

The City by the Bay
Urbs Iuxta Sinum

La-La Land
Terra La-La

The Mile-High City
Urbs Mille Passus Alta

Motown
Municipium Machinosum

The Quad Cities
Urbes Quadruplices

Sin City
Urbs Peccatorum

Tinsel Town
Oppidum Bracteatum

The Twin Cities
Urbes Geminae

The Windy City
Urbs Ventosa

LATIN: THE UNIVERSAL DIALECT

THE COAST

I'm sorry, Officer—I didn't know these freeways had no-smoking lanes.

- *Eius me paenitet, Aedilis. Nescivi has vias magnas habere straturas separatas in quibus non est fumandum.*

I'd like a hamburger, please, and hold the artichoke, avocado, lentils, tofu, and bean sprouts.

- *Da mihi, sodes, bubulae frustum assae, sed parce cinarae, perseae Americanae, lentibus, lacti concreto fabarum, et surculis phaselorum.*

That's nothing—in a previous life, I was a Roman emperor.

- *Nihil est—in vita priore ego imperator Romanus fui.*

THE PACIFIC NORTHWEST

Where's the Space Needle?

- *Ubi est Acus Caelestis?*

You say this is the world's first revolving restaurant?

- *Dicis in terris primam esse hanc cauponam quae se circumagit?*

So what can you see from up here when it isn't raining?

- *Quid autem potes hinc videre cum non pluit?*

THE SOUTH

Good to see y'all.

- *Mihi placet vos omnes videre.*

How're y'all doing?

- *Ut valetis, vos omnes?*

Y'all have a real fine day, y'hear?

- *Vos omnes die dulcissimo fruimini, auditisne?*

THE MIDWEST
Yes, that is a very large amount of corn.
- *Aio, quantitas magna frumentorum est.*

Do you pop it all here, or is that done somewhere else?
- *Hicine omnia dirumpis, an alibi?*

Tell me, how far *can* the eye actually see?
- *Dic mihi, quatenus re vera oculus potest videre?*

THE NORTHEAST
You talking to me?
- *Memetne adloqueris?*

Hey, you got a problem, pal?
- *Heia, comes, num aliquid agitur?*

Fuh-get about it.
- *Illius obli-viscere.*

CANADA
I have never seen cheese prepared so many different ways.
- *Nunquam visi caseum in tantis modis diversis paratum.*

My, this certainly is a clean city.
- *Mehercle, haec urbs pura est.*

It's a very neat city, too.
- *Haec urbs praeterea mundulissima est.*

UPDATED STATE MOTTOES

STATE	OLD MOTTO	NEW MOTTO
Arizona	*Deus Ditat* God enriches	*Deus, Aestuat* God, it's hot
California	*Eureka!* I found it!	*Caseum Caprinum in Eo Imposui!* I put goat cheese on it!
Colorado	*Nil Sine Numine* Nothing without Providence	*Nil Sine Nivibus* Nothing without snow
Connecticut	*Qui Transtulit, Sustinet* He who transplanted, sustains	*Qui Festinat, Castigatur* He who speeds, get nailed
Kansas	*Ad Astra, Per Aspera* To the stars, through difficulty	*Ad Aeroportum Propera* To the airport, and step on it
Maine	*Dirigo* I direct	*Te Derigam ad Fabam L.L.* I'll show you how to get to L.L. Bean
Massachusetts	*Ense Petit Placidam, sub Libertate Quietem* With a sword he seeks peace, but peace with liberty	*Anxie Stationem Petit, sed Non in Area unde Detrahatur* Eagerly he seeks a parking place, but not in a tow-away zone

Michigan	*Si Quaeris Peninsulam Amoenam, Circumspice* If you seek a pleasant peninsula, look around	*Si Quaeris Sanus Hinc Abire, Circumspice* If you want to get out of here alive, keep your eyes open
Missouri	*Salus Populi Suprema Lex Esto* The welfare of the people shall be the highest law	*Potus Populi Cerevesiarum Rex Est* The beverage of the people is Bud
New Mexico	*Crescit Eundo* It grows as it goes	*Omnia Venundo* It's all for sale
New York	*Excelsior!* Higher!	*Exactiones Excelsiores!* Higher taxes!
North Carolina	*Esse Non Videri* To be, not to seem	*Fumare Te Oportet* It behooves you to smoke
South Carolina	*Dum Spiro, Spero* While I breathe, I hope	*Hic Transiit Gloria* The hurricane came through here
Virginia	*Sic Semper Tyrannis* Thus always to tyrants	*Ite ad Infernos, Ianquii* Go to hell, Yankees

V.
INTERNATIONAL LATIN
Lingua Latina Foris

AT THE AIRPORT

How long will the flight be delayed?
- *Quanta mora volatui fiet?*

What do you mean, you're overbooked?
- *Ain, supra modum sedes conductae sunt?*

Is there a way to get there without going through Atlanta?
- *Potestne illuc pervenire Atlantam tamen praeteriens?*

Do I get frequent-flier miles for the walk between gates?
- *Daturne praemium plurima milia passuum volandi mihi tantum spatium gresso inter portas?*

How about an upgrade?
- *Velisne me extollere ad cursum pretiosiorem?*

Stand aside, plebians! I am on imperial business!
- *Recedite, plebes! Gero rem imperialem!*

ON AN AIRPLANE

Will this seat go back any further?
- *Haecine sedes potest ultro reclinari?*

No, I don't want a red-hot towelette.
- *Minime! Nolo mantele candens.*

Is *Pet Health* the only magazine you have?
- *Estne* Valetudo Animalium Domesticorum *periodicus libellus solus quem ad manum habes?*

What is the movie on this flight?
- *Quis est cinematographia in hoc volatu?*

And you expect me to pay for the headphones?
- *Et credisne me empturum esse conchas soniferas?*

I'll have a Bloody Mary, please.
- *Velim sumere Mariam Sanguinariam, sis.*

Could you get that baby to shut up?
- *Potesne compescere ululatum istius infantis?*

Don't you have anything besides Salisbury Steak and Chicken Cacciatore?
- *Nonne alium cibum habes praeter Bubulam Sorbiodunensem et Pullum Coctum Modo Venatoris?*

Hey, you've been in there for twenty minutes.
- *Heia, viginti iam minutos in latrina ines.*

Yeah, it was a great flight. Now where do I go to get branded and have my hooves dipped?
- *Sic, volatus praestat. Nunc quo vadam ut nota in me inuratur et ungulae medicamentis mergantur?*

AT THE RENTAL-CAR COUNTER

I don't want a subcompact.
- *Nolo cisium exiguum.*

I reserved a midsize.
- *Currum medium conduxi.*

Does this insurance cover me if I get sideswiped by some bastard in a chariot with knives on its wheels?
- *Subveniatne mihi haec fides damni resarciendi interposita si deiciar a nescio quo furcifero agente currum armatum defixis ad rotas cultris?*

THINGS TO SAY ON A CRUISE SHIP

I hate shuffleboard.
- *Ludum tabulaticum odi.*

What time is lunch?
- *Quando prandimus?*

Hey, Captain, why don't you open her up and see what this baby can do?
- *Agedum, Magister, habenas dans monstra quam velociter hic phaselus currere possit!*

How do you say "Man overboard!" in English?
- *Quomodo dicitur Anglice "Vir in mare excidit!"?*

Are we sinking?
- *Summergimurne?*

Women, children, and Latin speakers first!
- *Feminae, infantes atque illi qui Latine loqui possint antecedant!*

Making New Friends in Foreign Lands

SOUTH OF THE BORDER:
How come no one here speaks Latin? This is Latin America, isn't it?

- *Quapropter non adsunt qui Latine loquantur? Nonne est haec America Latina?*

ENGLAND:
Yeah? Well, how's *your* empire doing these days, smarty-pants?

- *Sic? Quomodonam se habet hodiernis diebus imperium tuum, salse bracate?*

FRANCE:
You know, you're not really speaking good French yourself—you're just badly mispronouncing lower-class provincial Latin.

- *Vero, tute reapse non bene loqueris Gallice—immo vero modo male et corrupte pronuntias sermonem Latinum plebium ac vernaculum.*

GERMANY:
So, who have you guys got lined up for your next world war?

- *Quos populos habetis in animo debellare proximo bello inter omnes gentes?*

ITALY:
Sheesh, have you let this place go downhill in the last two thousand years!

- *Mehercle, quantum sivistis hunc locum squalere annis proximis duobus milibus!*

SPAIN:

Look, why don't you throw a few Christians in there and let the bull win once in a while?

- *Ecce, inmitte sis in amphitheatrum paucos Christianos et permitte tauro aliquando vincere.*

AUSTRALIA:

G'day, mate. Will you please put another shrimp on the barbie for me?

- *Salve, socie. Pone mihi, sodes, alteram locustam marinam in caminello.*

THINGS TO SAY ON THE ORIENT EXPRESS

Quick, pretend you know me!
- *Cito, simula me cognoscere!*

See that man? He's a spy for the German tribes.
- *Videsne illum? Explorator Germanicus est.*

I have the plans for the new multiple independently targeted, boulder-hurling catapult. *Shhh!*
- *Descriptiones habeo catapultae novae quae saxos multos separatim et simul iaciant. St!*

If he gets his hands on them, it will be the end of the world as we know it.
- *Si illas prehendat, sit finis terrae qualem cognovimus.*

So, where are you headed?
- *Quo vadis?*

THINGS TO SAY IN A SIDEWALK CAFÉ

How are we to know whether we actually exist or only *think* we exist?
- *Quemadmodum possumus scire utrum vere simus an solum sentiamus nos esse?*

Can we ever truly distinguish art qua art from that which is merely pleasing to the eye?
- *Possumusne umquam vero artem ipsam secernere ab illis quae modo oculis grata sint?*

Could I get another cup of this great cappuccino and one of those little chocolate pastries?
- *Da mihi, sodes, alterum poculum huius capucincti suavissimi et unum e crustulis illis theobromaticis.*

You Sound Less Like a Tourist When You Gawk in Latin

Boy, if these old walls could talk!
* *Edepol, utinam hi parietes veteres dicere possint!*

How much do you think a painting like that would set you back?
* *Quanto credis picturam illius notae tibi staturam?*

If you sit on one of those chairs with a little rope across it, do you get a shock?
* *Si quis in unam ex illis sedibus, quibus funiculus est impositus, adsidat, cadat quasi fulmine stratus?*

That's the biggest bed I've ever seen.
* *Ille lectus est quem maximum vidi.*

How would you like to have a layout like this?
* *Nonne velis possidere latifundium similem huius?*

You could put a satellite dish on that turret.
* *Possis, si velis, in illa turricula ponere lancem ad stellas mechanicas auscultandas.*

There's enough room here for an eighteen-hole golf course.
* *Hic satis est spatium cursui ludi paganici Caledonii foraminum duodeviginti.*

But I bet the taxes and upkeep are murder.
* *Sed reor exactiones et impensas mortiferas esse.*

I wonder where the gift shop is.
* *Scire velim ubi taberna munusculorum sit.*

FOOD FOR THOUGHT: ROMANCE LANGUAGE MENU ALERT

horse	*caballus*
goat	*capra*
rabbit	*cuniculus*
brains	*cerebelli*
eel	*anguilla*
sea eels	*congri*
sea snails	*bucina*
sea slugs	*limaces*
lampreys	*lampredae*

Latin Is Always Acceptable in Polite Company

Who cut the cheese?
* *Quisnam pepedit!*

Catch that and sew a button on it!
* *Illud cape et ei fibulam adfige!*

Excuse me, I've got to go take a dump.
* *Ignosce mihi, cacare necesse est.*

Look out, I'm going to barf!
* *Cave, vomiturus sum!*

The Expletives Never Need to Be Deleted in Latin

You've got *stercus* for brains.

You are a complete and total *podex*.

Tete futue and the horse you rode in on.

THE FINE PRINT IS EVEN FINER IN LATIN

Batteries not included.
- *Lagunculae Leydianae non accedunt.*

Void where prohibited by law.
- *Inritum est qua legibus prohibitum est.*

Some restrictions may apply.
- *Forsitan ad hoc aliquot condiciones pertineant.*

Substantial penalty for early withdrawal.
- *Poenas magnas ob depositum praemature postulatum expetimus.*

A CHECKERED PAST IS EASIER TO REVEAL IN LATIN

I've been married before.
- *Matrimonio priore cum altera olim iunctus sum.*

This isn't my real name.
- *Hoc nomen meum verum non est.*

I spent some time in prison.
- *Spatium temporis in carcere egi.*

I don't really know all that much Latin.
- *Re vera, linguam Latinam vix cognovi.*

WIRETAPPERS DON'T KNOW LATIN

Whaddya say we bump him off?
- *Placetne tibi ut eum necemus?*

Let's stick up the joint.
- *Locum despoliemus.*

I got the stuff—you got the money?
- *Materiem habeo—habesne nummos?*

Swell! Hey, you know what I'm gonna do? I'm gonna evade all the income taxes on it!
- *Bene! At scin quid faciam? Certum est mihi subterfugere omnia vectigalia ei imposita!*

PILLOW TALK IS MORE ORIGINAL IN LATIN

How was it for you?
- *Quantum placui tibi?*

Did the earth move?
- *Movitne terra, ut ita dicam?*

Was I great, or what?
- *Nonne fui magnificus?*

Want to do it again?
- *Visne iterum agere?*

THINGS YOU SAY IN YOUR SLEEP SOUND LESS RIDICULOUS IN LATIN

I forgot to polish the clocks!
- *Oblitus sum perpolire clepsydras!*

Where's my rubber ducky?
- *Ubi est mea anaticula cumminosa?*

Uh-oh, here comes the lobster man!
- *Eheu, horsum venit vir qui fert locustas!*

Shower shoes! Shower shoes! Shower shoes!
- *Crepidae balneariae! Crepidae balneariae! Crepidae balneariae!*

CERTAIN REQUESTS ARE MORE TACTFULLY COMMUNICATED IN LATIN

Bite my crank.
- *Morde manubrium meum.*

Eat my shorts.
- *Vescere bracis meis.*

Put it where the sun don't shine.
- *Pone ubi sol non lucet.*

TERMS OF NONENDEARMENT

Airhead
Caput vacans

Bimbo
Muliercula

Buttface
Vultus natiformis

Cheese dong
Praeputium

Creep
Cimex

Dolt
Vervex

Doofus
Blennus

Dork
Caudex

Mouthbreather
Hiator

Numbnuts
Testibus torpidis

Sleazeball
Pila foeda

Space cadet
Tiro in exercitu stellarum

Turboslut
Moecha mobilis

Wannabe
Simulator

VII.
GENERAL LATIN
Lingua Latina Generalis

A Latin Chain Letter

This letter has been around the known world many times, and it brings luck wherever it goes. Make ten copies and send them to your friends. Do not break the chain. A person in France broke the chain, and soon after his country was divided into three parts. A general in the Philistines forgot about the letter, and his forces were routed. But Scipio Africanus sent copies of this letter to all the senators in Rome, and the next day he defeated the Carthaginians. Good luck!

• *Haec epistula orbem terrarum cognitarum saepenumero curcumiit et fortunam secundam fert ubicumque eat. Decem exemplaria fac et eos mitte ad amicos. Noli catenam frangere. Homo Gallicus catenam fregit, et patria sua in tres partes brevi post divisa est. Dux ex Philistinis epistulam dedidicit, et copiae suae fusae sunt. Sed Scipio Africanus, exemplaribus epistulae ad senatores Romanos omnes missis, die proximo Carthaginienses vicit. Bona fortuna!*

A Latin Sign for Your Office Desk

COGGITE.

• THIMK.

AN ALL-PURPOSE GET-WELL NOTE

I just want you to know that I have sacrificed a good-sized she-goat to Mercury on your behalf in order to hasten your recovery.
PS The entrails were auspicious!
PPS Get well soon!

Volo te scire me capram magnam Mercurio sacrificavisse pro salute tuo celerius restituendo.
PS Exta fausta fuerunt!
PPS Convalesce velociter!

DOCTORS' NOTES ARE MORE CONVINCING IN LATIN

To whom it may concern:
This patient is very sick. He should not go to work under any circumstances. If he feels up to it, he may play a round or two of golf each day, or engage in some similar low-stress activity. He will recover fully, but it's going to take quite some time.

Ei cuius interest:
Hic gravissimo morbo adficitur. Eum oportet haudquaquam laborare. Si se paululum sentiat valescere, ludere lusum Caledonium semel bisve per diem, aut re simili sine sudore operave possit perfungi. E morbo omnino convalescet, sed sibi multo temporis opus erit.

An All-Purpose Letter to the Editor

Dear Blockhead:

Your publication is a scandalous waste of animal hides and papyrus reeds, and your views are unworthy of even the lowliest rabble. If I were emperor (and it may interest you to know that in a previous life I *was*), you'd be sent into exile and spend the rest of your miserable days scribbling bitter diatribes on bits of bark in a smelly hovel in Dalmatia.

Care Baro:

Libellus tuus est iactura probosa pellium papyrique et sententiae tuae indignae etiam plebecula humillima sunt. Si imperator essem (qualis vita priore fui, *ut tua fortasse intersit cognoscere), tum tu eiectus in exilium vitam reliquam miserrime degeres scribens Philippicas acerbas in frusta corticis in gurgustio male olenti apud Dalmatas.*

AN ALL-PURPOSE RESPONSE TO DUNNING LETTERS FROM SCHOOLS

Dear Sirs:

As you can no doubt tell from my superb Latin, I have dedicated my life to the study of the classics, which, as you probably know, is not a major money-making occupation. Consequently, I am not now, nor will I ever be, able to send you any money. I am certain, however, that any disappointment you might feel at this turn of events is more than compensated for by the great pride you surely have in the scholarly commitment of a former student.

PS Are your diplomas still in Latin?

PPS I think there's a wrong ending in a word in our Latin school motto.

Cari Amici:

Quod haud dubie fit vobis certum ex hac epistula tam eleganter Latine scripta, me dedicavi ad studium litterarum antiquarum, quae, ut fortasse scias bene, negotium non sane quaestuosum est. Ergo, nunc non possum nec umquam potero vobis reddere ullam pecuniam. Pro certo habeo, autem, quemquem dolorem ob illam rem sentiatis omnino compensatum esse ab aestimatione coeptorum eruditorum unius ex vestris discipulis prioribus.

PS Etiamnunc diplomata tua Latine scribuntur?

PPS Credo verbum in nostrae scholae sententia symbolica Latina in falso casu esse.

AN ALL-PURPOSE BEDTIME STORY

Once upon a time there were three bears who went for a walk in the woods while their porridge cooled. While they were away, a yellow-haired barbarian girl broke in, ate their food, busted their furniture, and slept in their beds, but when the bears came back, they made a slave of her, and she turned out to be very useful around the house. The end.

Olim erant tres ursi qui in silvas iverant ad ambulandum dum puls sua refrigescat. His absentibus, barbara flava inrupit, escam edit, supellectilem fregit, et in lectis dormivit. Sed cum ursi revenissent, eam in servitutem redegerunt, et ea postea utilissima domi fiebat. Finis.

A NOTE TO SANTA

Dear Santa,
I would like a Rolex wristwatch, four Armani suits, and a Ferrari. Thank you.
PS I can name all your reindeer in Latin: Blitzen, Comet, Cupid, Dancer, Dasher, Donder, Prancer, Vixen, and Rudolph the Red-Nosed.

Care Sancte Nicholas,
Aveo horologium manuale Rolicis, quattuor vestitus Armanios, et currum a Ferrario factum. Tibi gratias ago.
PS Scio nomina Latina rangiferorum tuorum omnium: Fulgens, Cometes, Cupido, Saltator, Provolans, Tonitrus, Exsultans, Vulpes, et Rudolphus Naso Rubro.

Ann N. Graham
her book

HANDY ACRONYMS FROM THE LAND OF SPQR

KISS   Keep It Simple, Stupid
- *SSS   Sit Simplex, Stulte*

CYA   Cover Your Ass
- *PTP   Protege Tuam Pugam*

NIMBY   Not In My Backyard
- *NPIMV   Ne Ponatur In Mea Vicinitate*

MEGO   My Eyes Glaze Over
- *OMFL   Oculi Mei Fiunt Languidi*

LITTLE LEAGUE LATIN

We want a pitcher, not a glass of water!
- *Egemus iaculatore, non iacchi latore!*

Swings like a rusty gate!
- *Agitat instar ianuae robiginosae!*

He couldn't hit his baby brother!
- *Fratrem parvulum non potest ferire!*

Swing, batter!
- *Pelle, percutor!*

Strike out!
- *Eliditur!*

Latin Chatter for the Infield

Whaddya say, whaddya say, whaddya say!
- *Quid dicis, quid dicis, quid dicis!*

Come on, baby, come on, baby!
- *Age, bone, age, bone!*

Put it in there, put it in there!
- *Ibi id impone, ibi id impone!*

Hey hey, say say!
- *Sic sic, dic dic!*

Easy out, easy out, easy out!
- *Exactio facilis, exactio facilis, exactio facilis!*

No batter, no batter, no batter!
- *Nihil tundit, nihil tundit, nihil tundit!*

All right, all right! Way to go, way to go!
- *Bene, bene! Eugepae, eugepae!*

LATIN CHEERS FOR THE IVY LEAGUE

Pursue them, pursue them, make them relinquish the ball!
- *Sequimini, sequimini, facite ut pilam relinquant!*

Repel them, expel them, compel them to retreat!
- *Illos repellite, expellite, compellite ad fugiendum!*

Oh, would that we would score!
- *Utinam vincamus!*

We have been wanting and shall continue to want a touch-down!
- *Volebamus atque volemus pilam trans metas deponi!*

Just like Gaul, just like Gaul, divide them up into three separate parts, just like Gaul!
- *Sicut Gallia, Sicut Gallia, illi vobis in tres partes dividendi sunt!*

ENCOURAGE THE HOME TEAM WITH WELL-CHOSEN IMPERATIVES

ALABAMA:
Crimson Tide—"Roll, Tide, roll!"
- *Aestus maritimus coccineus—"Surge, Volve, aestus!"*

ARKANSAS:
Razorbacks—"Woo, pig soooey!"
- *Porci—"Eu, sues, suilli!"*

GEORGIA TECH:
Yellowjackets—"I'm a rambling wreck from Georgia Tech!"
- *Vespidae—"Sum naufragium vagans de collegio Georgiae Technologico!"*

NOTRE DAME:
Fighting Irish—"Cheer, cheer, for old Notre Dame!"
- *Hibernici Pugnaces—"Io! Io! Domina Nostra venerabilis!"*

CLASSICAL CHEERS FOR YOUR LOCAL COLOSSEUM

DEEE-fense!
- *DeFENNNN-sio!*

AAAAASSSSSS-hole!
- *CUUUUUUU-le!*

Two, four, six, eight—who do we appreciate?
- *Duo, quattor, sex, octo—cui multum tribuimus?*

Na-na-na-na, na-na-na-na, hey-hey-hey, good-bye!
- *Nae-nae-nae-nae, nae-nae-nae-nae, heia-heia, vale!*

Support Your Local Gladiators

Here we go, (your team), here we go!
- *Progrediamur, (manus cui faves), progrediamur!*

AFC EAST

Buffalo Bills	*Gulielmi Bovarii*
Indianapolis Colts	*Eculei Indianapolitani*
Miami Dolphins	*Delphines Miamiae*
New England Patriots	*Amantes Patriae Novae Angliae*
New York Jets	*Effunditores Novi Eboraci*

AFC CENTRAL

Cincinnati Bengals	*Tigres Indici Cincinnati*
Cleveland Browns	*Fusci Clevelandenses*
Houston Oilers	*Olearii Houstoni*
Pittsburgh Steelers	*Chalybes Pittsburgenses*

AFC WEST

Denver Broncos	*Equi Feri Denverae*
Kansas City Chiefs	*Principes Urbis Kansatis*
Los Angeles Raiders	*Latrones Municipii Angelorum*
San Diego Chargers	*Impetitores Sancti Iacobi*
Seattle Seahawks	*Haliaeti Seattlenses*

NFC EAST

Dallas Cowboys	*Vaccatores Dallati*
New York Giants	*Gigantes Noveboracenses*
Philadelphia Eagles	*Aquilae Philadelphiae*
Phoenix Cardinals	*Cardinales Phoenices*
Washington Redskins	*Rubripelles Washingtonenses*

NFC CENTRAL

Chicago Bears	*Ursi Chicagonenses*
Detroit Lions	*Leones Fretenses*
Green Bay Packers	*Baiuli Sinus Viridis*
Minnesota Vikings	*Viri Normani Minnesotae*
Tampa Bay Buccaneers	*Praedones Maritimi Tampaenses*

NFC WEST

Atlanta Falcons	*Falcones Atlantae*
Los Angeles Rams	*Arietes Municipii Angelorum*
New Orleans Saints	*Sancti Novaurelianenses*
San Francisco 49ers	*Undequinquaginti Sancti Francisci*

IX.
ESSENTIAL LATIN
Lingua Latina Necessaria

Chance Encounters Are Less Awkward in Latin

Look what the cat dragged in!
- *Aspice quod felis attraxit!*

Long time no see!
- *Tam diu minime visu!*

Where have you been hiding yourself?
- *Ubi tete occultabas?*

Let's not be strangers!
- *Non simus inter nos advenas!*

See you later, alligator!
- *Vale, lacerte!*

Don't do anything I wouldn't do!
- *Noli aliquid facere quod non faciam!*

Jeepers, what a ying-yang!
- *Edepol, qualem praeputium!*

You Always Have a Leg Up in Latin

I'd like the usual Vatican discount.
- *Volo id ex pretio decrescere quod solet cum Vaticanum negotietur.*

Hi. I'm here to pick up the pope's Super Bowl tickets.
- *Ave. Hic adsum ad tesseras pontificis maximi Colosseo Maximo tollendas.*

We'll need an earlier tee time. The archbishop has to get back to the cathedral to judge the Gregorian chant sing-off.
- *Necesse est nobis maturius incipere a "Te." Archiepiscopus debet redire ad ecclesiam cathedralem ut iudicet certamen cantus Gregoriani.*

Affirmations Are More Affirmative in Latin

I'm not just whistling "Dixie"!
- *Non modo sibilo "Terram Dixonis!"*

Does a bear shit in the woods?
- *Cacatne ursus in sylvis?*

Does the pope speak Latin?
- *Loquiturne pontifex maximus Latine?*

Word!
- *Verbum!*

Rationalizations Are More Rational in Latin

If I hadn't done it, someone else would have.
- *Si id non fecissem, aliquis id fecisset.*

Everyone does it.
- *Sic faciunt omnes.*

What they don't know won't kill them.
- *Quod nesciunt eos non interficiet.*

So what's it to you, anyway?
- *Num curae est tibi?*

A Good Defense Is Even Better in Latin

I don't know what you're talking about.
- *Nescio de quo loqueris.*

There's obviously been some sort of silly mistake.
- *Manifesto nescio quis lapsus stultus factus est.*

You must be mad.
- *Vere furis.*

Is this your idea of a joke?
- *Hocine tibi habeas iocum?*

Can you actually prove any of that?
- *Potesne vere ullam partem probare?*

That's my story, and I'm sticking to it.
- *Quae narravi, nullo modo negabo.*

Comebacks Are Snappier in Latin

Says who?
- *Quis est qui inquit?*

Is that a fact?
- *Vere dicis?*

T.S.!
- *D.M.!*

So's your old man!
- *Atque vetulus tuus!*

Put-Downs Are More Final in Latin

Who rattled your cage?
- *Quis caveam tuam quassit?*

Well, pardon me for living.
- *Vae, da mihi veniam vitae.*

Get a life.
- *Fac ut vivas.*

Be real.
- *Veritatem imitare.*

Wake up and smell the coffee.
- *Expergiscere et coffeam olface.*

TALK IS NEVER CHEAP IN LATIN

You're dead meat.
- *Caro putrida es.*

You'll never work in this town again.
- *In hoc oppido nunquam postea operaberis.*

You can run, but you can't hide.
- *Potes currere, sed te occulere non potes.*

Guys like you are a dime a dozen.
- *Capita similia tui aestimantur unius assis.*

I have jerks like you for breakfast.
- *Verveces tui similes pro ientaculo mihi appositi sunt.*

Read it and weep.
- *Lege et lacrima.*

Don't make me laugh.
- *Ne feceris ut rideam.*

I'm shaking, I'm shaking.
- *Pavesco, pavesco.*

Snow Jobs Are Howling Blizzards in Latin

You look marvelous!
- *Quam pulcher/pulchra es!*

How truly fascinating! Do tell me more!
- *Tua verba animum meum tenent! Te precor mihi plus enarrare!*

That's simply divine!
- *Divinissimum est!*

I had a grand time!
- *Me valde oblectavi.*

I shall always cherish the memory of this very, very special occasion.
- *Semper redibo laetus hunc diem praecipuum in memoriam.*

Perhaps a small obelisk could be erected to commemorate it.
- *Forsitan nobis deceat statuere obeliscum parvum ad rem celebrandam.*

You Can Sell Practically Anybody Practically Anything in Latin

Tell you what I'm going to do . . .
- *Mihi permitte tibi dicere quod faciam . . .*

This is a rock-bottom price.
- *Hoc est pretium minimum.*

I'm losing money on this deal.
- *Hoc pacto, pecuniam amitto.*

My boss will kill me when he finds out.
- *Praefectus me e medio tollet quando cognoverit.*

Sign here.
- *Hic signa.*

Next!
- *Propinqua proxime!*

Latin: The Mother of All Tongues

First we're going to cut it off, then we're going to kill it.
- *Primum id abscidemus, tum id occidemus.*

He didn't move it, and now he's going to lose it.
- *Illud non movit, ergo illud perdet.*

I came, I saw, I kicked ass.
- *Veni, vidi, nates calce concidi.*

X.
POP-CULTURAL LATIN
Lingua Latina Popularis

ALL COMICS ARE CLASSIC COMICS IN LATIN

It's a bird! It's a plane! It's Superman!
- *Avis est! Aeronavis est! Supervir est!*

Holy subjunctives, Batman!
- *Sanctos subiunctivos, Virvespertilio!*

Oh no, Spidey's having an identity crisis!
- *Eheu, Araneus dubitat qui ipse sit!*

The Hulk broke up with his girlfriend!
- *Moles familiaritatem sibi cum amica dirupit!*

Shazam!
- *Hercule!*

CARTOONS ARE, WELL, CARTOONIER IN LATIN

What's up, Doc?
- *Quid agis, Medice!*

I'll get you, you wascally wabbit!
- *Te capiam, cunicule sceleste!*

I tought I taw a puddy tat!
- *Credidi me felem vidisse!*

Thuffering Thuccotash!
- *Farrago fatigans!*

Beep-beep!
- *Cornu sono!*

Ah-bee, ah-bee, ah-bee, that's all, folks!
- *Abeo, abeo, abeo, actum est, comites!*

THE GOLDEN AGE OF TV WOULD HAVE BEEN EVEN MORE GOLDEN IN LATIN

Just the facts, ma'am.
• *Dic mihi solum facta, domina.*

Sorry about that, chief.
• *Illius me paenitet, dux.*

You bet your bippy!
• *Tuis pugis pignore!*

The devil made me do it!
• *Diabolus fecit, ut id facerem!*

Kiss my grits!
• *Osculare pultem meam!*

Beam me up, Scotty!
• *Me transmitte sursum, Caledoni!*

If you fail, the secretary will disavow all knowledge of your activities.
• *Si fallatis officium, quaestor infitias eat se quicquam scire de factis vestris.*

You'd Have Been Allowed to Listen to the Radio All Night If Only It Had Been in Latin

What's behind that creaking door?
- *Quid pone illud ostium crepans situm est?*

The Shadow knows.
- *Umbra scit.*

Who was that masked man?
- *Quis fuit ille personatus?*

Hi-ho, Silver, away!
- *Eeia, Argentei, eamus!*

Good night, Mrs. Calabash, wherever you are.
- *Vale, era Curcurbita, ubicumque sis.*

THE ALL-TIME TOP X

I Heard It Through the Grapevine
- *Hoc Fama Mihi, Cursum Sinuosum Secuta, Nuntiat*

Itsy Bitsy Teeny Weenie Yellow Polka Dot Bikini
- *Ceston atque Cingulum Parvissimos Minutissimos Natatorios Flavos Ocellatos*

The 59th Street Bridge Song (Feelin' Groovy)
- *Cantus Pontis Viae Undesexagesimae (Laetans)*

Stop in the Name of Love
- *Siste in Nomine Amoris*

Shake, Rattle, and Roll
- *Treme, Strepe, et Volutare*

These Boots Are Made for Walking
- *Caligae ad Ambulandum Factae Sunt*

Be True to Your School
- *Fidelis Scholae Tuae Esto*

You Can't Always Get What You Want
- *Non Potes Semper Capere Quod Aves*

Diamonds on the Soles of Her Shoes
- *Sunt Adamantes in Solis Calceorum Suorum*

Everybody's Got Something to Hide Except for Me and My Monkey
- *Habent Abdenda Omnes Praeter Me ac Simiam Meam*

WRITE YOUR OWN LATIN B-MOVIE SCRIPT

Huge flying discuses have landed in the Campus Martius!
- *Orbes immanes volantes in Campum Martium advenerunt!*

It's horrible! These creatures have the head of a lizard and the body of a Helvetian!
- *Horribile dictu! His animalibus biformibus sunt caput lacerti iunctum ad corpus Helvetii!*

Our weapons are useless against them!
- *Tela nostra nihil nobis prosunt in illos.*

Send for the Greek thinker! Perhaps he can save us with his arcane arts!
- *Arcesse Palameden! Forsitan possit nos servare artibus suis abditis!*

It's MMMMMMM to I, but it's our only chance—a flame-hurling catapult!
- *Cum sit periculum tremendum, res tamen in aleam nobis danda est—ecce catapulta quae liquorem ardentem iacit!*

It's so crazy it just might work!
- *Tam insulsum est ut fortasse expediat.*

Incredible! The Greek fire is melting them like wax!
- *Incredibile est! Ignis Graecus illos dissolvit quasi e cera facti sint!*

Is it The End, or The Beginning of The End, or The End of The Beginning, or The Beginning . . . ?
- *Estne Finis, aut Initium Finis, aut Finis Initii, aut Initium . . . ?*

The Seven Dwarfs Gain More Stature in Latin

Dopey
Fatuus

Doc
Medicullus

Grumpy
Severus

Happy
Beatus

Sleepy
Somniculosus

Bashful
Verecundus

Sneezy
Sternuens

Nostalgia Is More Nostalgic in Latin

Let's have a Tupperware party!
• *Habeamus convivium ad mercem emendam Tupperi!*

Let's turn on the lava lamp!
• *Accendamus lucernam plenam massae ardentis!*

Let's all wear mood rings!
• *Anulos qui animum ostendunt omnes gestemus!*

Let's have a sock hop!
• *In tibialibus saltemus!*

Immortal Headlines from *The Classical Enquirer*

PUER PATREM CAEDIT, MATREM SUAM IN MATRIMONIUM DUCIT
- YOUTH KILLS HIS DAD, MARRIES OWN MOM

*CUM BELUA BARBARA IN LABYRINTHO NEFANDO PUGNAT: SEMIVIR,
   SEMIBOS CARNEM HUMANAM EDIT*
- HE BATTLES WEIRD BEAST IN HELLISH MAZE: HALF-MAN, HALF-BULL
   DINED ON HUMAN FLESH

*REX DEMENS INFANTES FRATRIS SUI INTERFICIT COQUITQUE, TUM
   CENAM FOEDAM PARENTI HORRIFICATO APPONIT*
- MAD KING SLAYS AND COOKS HIS BROTHER'S TOTS, THEN SERVES
   LOATHSOME DISH TO TYKES' HORRIFIED POP

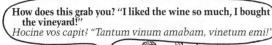

BE YOUR OWN AD EXEC WITH LINGO FROM THE VIA MADISONIS

Let's run it up the flagpole and see if anybody salutes it!
- *Id in summum longurium quasi vexillum tollamus ut videamus utrum quis id salutet, necne!*

Let's put it in the Colosseum and see if the lions will eat it!
- *Id in Colosseo ponamus ut videamus utrum leones id edant, necne!*

Let's divide it into three parts and see if anybody conquers it!
- *Id in tres partes dividamus ut videamus utrum quis id vincat, necne!*

Let's make it emperor and see if anybody assassinates it in the Forum!
- *Id imperatorem faciamus ut videamus utrum quis in Foro id interficiat, necne!*

Immortal Tag Lines Are Even More Classic in Latin

It takes a tough man to make a tender chicken.
- *Solus fortis et durus pullum tenerum parare potest.*

Tastes great! Less filling!
- *Iucunde sapit! Minime implet!*

I can't believe I ate the whole thing.
- *Non possum credere me totum edisse.*

It's ugly, but it gets you there.
- *Deformis est, sed te illuc fert.*

Where's the beef?
- *Ubi est bubula?*

Moronic Tag Lines Are Slightly More Bearable in Latin

Please don't squeeze the Charmin!
- *Sis, noli Volvivoluptatem comprimere!*

It's the quicker picker-upper.
- *Tollit velocius.*

I liked the shaver so much, I bought the company.
- *Tantum novaculam amabam, societatem emi.*

My wife—I think I'll keep her.
- *Uxor mea—Credo me eam semper retenturum.*

Just do it.
- *Modo fac.*

THE OLDEST JINGLES SOUND BRAND-NEW IN LATIN

Double your pleasure, double your fun, with double good, double fresh Doublemint gum!
- *Duplica gaudia tua et delectamenta, bis bona, bis nova, gummi Diplomentha!*

Hold the pickles, hold the lettuce! Special orders don't upset us, at McDonald's!
- *Parce cucumeris frustis! Parce lactucae! Mandata peculiaria nobis non sunt oneri, apud Filium Donaldi!*

Call Roto-Rooter—that's the name—and away go troubles down the drain!
- *Vocate Purgatorem Versabundum—nomen est nobis—et in cloacas abluemus calamitates quae sunt vobis!*

Gaudeat Emptor! (Let the Buyer Rejoice!)

Shake 'n Bake
Quate et Coque

Roast'n Boast
Torre ac Gloriare

Pop Tarts
Scriblitae Exsilientes

Devil Dogs
Crusti Diaboli

Rice-a-Roni
Oryza Mixta

Tuna Helper
Adiutor Thunni

Fish sticks
Piscilli

Sloppy Joes
Iosephi Inconditi

Fig Newtons
Crustuli Ficulnei

Chips Ahoy
Ave Assulae

Handy Wipes
Mantelia Habilia

Ty-D-Bol
Matula Nitida

Sweet 'n Low
Dulce Leveque

Tender Vittles
Esca Tenera

Kibbles 'n' Bits
Frusti et Gustuli

Pampers
Indulgentes

Miracle Whip
Confusio Mirifica

Roach Motels
Cauponae Blattariae

Yard Guard
Custodia Propatuli

Jujubes
Zizypha

XII.
CELEBRATIONAL LATIN
Lingua Latina Festiva

THINGS TO SAY ON YOUR BIRTHDAY

Happy Birthday to me!
• *Diem natalem felicem mihi!*

For me? You shouldn't have!
• *Mihi? Opus non fuit!*

I never would have guessed!
• *Nunquam coniectaverim!*

It's just what I wanted!
• *Est admodum quod volui!*

Where on earth did you find it?
• *Ubi gentium illud invenisti?*

Do you happen to know offhand what their policy is on returns?
• *Scisne forte quid soleant agere cum res reductis?*

Things to Say at a Bar Mitzvah

This is delicious. What is it?
* *Iucunde sapit. Quid est?*

May I have some more smoked salmon?
* *Da mihi, sis, plus salmonis fumosi.*

Things to Say on Groundhog Day

How do you know you have the right groundhog?
* *Ut scis te observare marmotam monacem ipsam?*

What happens if he wanders out on a highway and gets run over by a truck? Do we get an ice age?
* *Quid fiat si in viam erret et a vehiculo magno conculcetur? Saeclum glaciale?*

Latin Valentines for St. Valentine's Day

Roses are red, violets are blue, Gaul is divided into three parts, And so will my heart be if I ever lose you!	*Rubore di tinxerunt rosas Caeruleo di tinxerunt violas Cor meum in partes tres dividatur si tu me umquam relinquas!*
Roses are red, violets are blue, I don't care if the Carthaginians keep Carthage, So long as I always have you!	*Rubore di tinxerunt rosas, Caeruleo di tinxerunt violas Ita Carthaginienses Carthaginem habere possint ut semper habeam meas delicias!*

THINGS TO SAY ON ST. PATRICK'S DAY

Erin, go bragh!
- *Hibernia in aeternum!*

If I drink this funny-looking beer, will my pee turn green, too?
- *Si bibam hanc cerevesiam, quae speciem insolitam praebet, urinane mea eveniet quoque viridans?*

May all your nouns and adjectives agree in gender and number. . . .
- *Nomina omnia et nomina adiectiva tua in genere et numero congruant. . . .*

May you always use the subjunctive properly. . . .
- *Modo subiunctivo recte utaris. . . .*

And may you never accidentally try out your Latin on a Jesuit.
- *Et casu Latine loqui cum sodale Societatis Jesu ne umquam conaris.*

THINGS TO SAY AT EASTER

If he's the Easter *Bunny*, where does he get the eggs?
- *Si* Cuniculus *Paschalis sit, unde ova capiat?*

Maybe they're really brought by the Easter Lizard or the Easter Snake.
- *Forsitan re ipsa Lacerta Paschalis vel Anguis Paschalis illa ferat.*

Handy Messages for Everyone's Least Favorite Holidays

Dear Mom:
I know I never write, I know I
never call,
I'm really most contrite, but
I've been very busy in Gaul.
Happy Mother's Day.

Cara mater mea:
Scio me tibi non unquam scri-
bere, scio me tibi non filo
dicere,
Huius me valde paenitebat,
sed mihi in Gallia opus erat.
Felici die maternali fruere.

Dear Dad:
I'm not too proud to pen it: You
never got your due.
That's why I've asked the Sen-
ate to name a salad for you.
Happy Father's Day.

Care pater mi:
Vere, id mihi scribendum est:
Multum tibi debendum est.
Igitur cogito Senatum rogare
acetaria ex te rite appellare.
Felici die paternali fruere.

Things to Say at Graduation

Hey, this diploma is in English!
• *Vae! Hoc diploma Anglice scriptum est!*

Gyp! Gyp! I want my money back!
• *Fraudem! Fraudem! Mea pecunia vobis redenda est!*

Things to Say on the Fourth of July

Wow! Did you see that one?
- *Hercle! Illud vidistine?*

Look! This one's going to be even bigger!
- *Aspice! Hoc etiam grandius erit!*

Oooooooooo!
- *Uuuuuuuuuu!*

Things to Say on Halloween

Trick or Treat!
- *Dolus vel dulce!*

Sorry, kids, all I have is olives and figs.
- *Mihi paenitet, pueri, sed nihil aliud habeo nisi olivas et ficos.*

What do you mean, "nice costume"? This is my best toga!
- *Quid vis dicere, "vestitus theatralis suavis"? Haec est mea toga optima!*

That mask isn't very scary. Have you ever seen a Helvetian?
- *Larva illa non est formidolosior. Umquam vidisti Helvetium?*

Do you know what a catapult is?
- *Novistisne quid sit catapulta?*

If you're thinking of putting toilet paper on my house, ask yourself if you can outrun a ninety-mile-an-hour rock.
- *Si in animis habeatis scidam latrinariam in domo mea ponere, vosmet rogate si possitis velocius currere quam saxum quod vadit cum celeritate nonaginta milia passuum per horam.*

Things to Say at Thanksgiving

I'd like to help, but I only know how to cut up birds for
purposes of augury.
- *Cum velim te iuvare, solum tamen scio aves secare ad
augurandum.*

What actually is the difference between a yam and a sweet
potato?
- *Quomodonam dioscorea et ipomoea inter se differunt?*

You know, we really ought to have turkey more often.
- *Opinor vere meleagridem gallopavonem nobis saepius edendum
esse.*

I'll have some more mashed potatoes and gravy.
- *Da mihi, amabo, plus solanorum tuberosorum tunsorum et iuris.*

Oh boy, pumpkin pie!
- *Euax, crustum cucurbitae peponis!*

Um, do you by any chance happen to have a vomitorium in
this house?
- *En, habeasne forte in hac domo vomitorium?*

Things to Say on Hanukkah

Happy Hanukkah!
- *Hanukka felicem vobis!*

So enough already with the Latin-Schmatin, let's eat.
- *Iam est satis superque linguae Latinae-Fatuinae. Edamus.*

Things to Say at Christmas

Bah! Humbug!
- *Phy! Fabulae!*

Christmas has gotten too commercial.
- *Dies natalis Christi nimis mercatoria facta est.*

I'll have some more of that eggnog.
- *Sumam plus oögalactos.*

So, who do you like for the Super Bowl?
- *Bene, cui in Colosseo Maximo faves!*

New Year's Resolutions Are Less Binding in Latin

This year I am definitely going to . . .
- *Hoc anno ego pro certo . . .*

> go on a diet.
> *diaetam sequi incipiam.*

> get more exercise.
> *musculos saepius exercebo.*

> attend more cultural events.
> *adsidue bonis artibus studere.*

> make larger charitable contributions.
> *liberalius largiar.*

> be nicer to people.
> *benignius aliis me geram.*

> stop misusing the subjunctive.
> *abuti modo subiunctivo desinam.*

A BRIEF GUIDE TO
LATIN PRONUNCIATION

Locutio Linguae Latinae Paucis Verbis Explanatur

If it's been a few years since you last conversed in Latin regularly, your pronunciation may have gotten a bit rusty, so we've included here a short summary of the basics of the spoken language just to help you brush up a little.

A word of caution: This is a simplified system of pronunciation for colloquial Latin based in part on modern Italian, the direct vernacular descendant of the everyday speech of ancient Rome. If you're planning to give a formal oration or a reading from one of the great works of classical literature, you're obviously going to want to consult the standard scholarly reference books for the proper literary pronunciation.

I VOWELS AND A FEW DIPHTHONGS

Sure, I speak a little Latin.
- *Sane, paululum linguae Latinae dico.*
  SAH-nay, pow-LOO-luhm LEEN-gwye Lah-TEE-nye DEE-koh.

A is pronounced "ah" as in "f<u>a</u>ther."

E is pronounced "ay" as in "th<u>ey</u>," but the very common words <u>et</u> (and), <u>est</u> (is), and <u>sed</u> (but) should be pronounced like "b<u>e</u>t," "b<u>e</u>st," and "s<u>ai</u>d," and the very common word ending <u>em</u> should be pronounced like "st<u>em</u>."

I   is pronounced "ee" as in "Vaseline," but the very common words id (it) and in (in, on) should be pronounced like "did" and "din."

O   is pronounced "oh" as in "go."

U   is pronounced "oo" as in "crude," but the very common word endings us and um should be pronounced like "puss" and "room" (with the "oo" sound of "cookbook"), and the very common word ut (how, so that) should be pronounced like "put."

AE   is a diphthong (a pair of vowels joined together to form a single sound) pronounced "eye."

AU   is a diphthong pronounced "ow," as in "luau."

OE   is a diphthong pronounced "oy."

II   CONSONANTS

I picked it up here and there. Really, Latin isn't all that hard.

• *Id legi modo hic modo illic. Vero, Latine loqui non est difficilius.*

IDD LAY-gee MOH-doh HEEK MOH-doh EEL-leek. WAY-roh, Lah-TEE-nay LOH-kwee NOHN EHSST dee-fee-KEE-lee-uss.

B, D, F, H, K, L, M, N, P, and Z all sound the same as they do in English.

C   always has a "K" sound as in "car."

Ch   always has a "K" sound as in "chorus."

G   always has a hard "G" sound as in "get."

Gu   is pronounced "Gw" when it comes after an "n," as it is in "language."

I   is a consonant pronounced like "Y" when it is the first letter in a word and it is followed by a vowel. The common Latin word iam (now) is pronounced "YAHM."

Qu   is pronounced "Kw," just as in English.

R   can be rolled in a sort of Scottish burr.

S   always has a hissing sound as in "moose" or "soda," and some very common word endings sound like this: <u>as</u> = "demitasse"; <u>es</u> = "<u>ace</u>"; <u>is</u> = "<u>geese</u>"; <u>os</u> = "verb<u>ose</u>"; and <u>us</u> = "w<u>uss</u>."

T   always has a hard "T" sound as in "tar." In Latin, the word "ratio" is pronounced "RAH-tee-oh."

V   is always pronounced as if it were a "W." What Caesar (KYE-sahr) said after he defeated somebody or other (*veni, vidi, vici*) sounded as if he had just conquered Hawaii: WAY-nee, WEE-dee, WEE-kee.*

X   is always pronounced "Ks."

J, W, and Y don't exist in Latin.

III SYLLABLES

It looks like a tricky language, but you'll get the hang of it pretty quickly.

• *Lingua speciem involutam praebet, sed sat cito eam comprehendes.*

LEEN-gwah SPAY-kee-ehm inn-woh-LOO-tahm PRYE-bayt, SEDD SAHT KEE-toh AY-ahm kohm-pray-HAYN-dace.

Latin words are divided into syllables in the same way that English words are, but in Latin every vowel or diphthong is a syllable, and every syllable is pronounced separately. If there are two vowels together, and they are not AE, AU, or OE, both vowels are pronounced individually. So, for example, <u>praebat</u> = "PRYE-baht" (ae is a diphthong); <u>speciem</u> = "SPAY-kee-ehm"; and <u>eam</u> = "AY-ahm."

---

* If you took Latin in a parochial school, you were probably taught to pronounce the letter "V" like the English "V," the dipthong "ae" like "sund<u>ae</u>", and Caesar like "CHAY-sahr." If you do this, you are going to take some flak from Latin purists, classics snobs, and other assorted lingo bores, but on the other hand, you're going to get a much better table in the Vatican restaurant.

IV STRESS

And remember, there aren't any Romans around to correct
  your pronunciation.
- *Atque memento, nulli adsunt Romanorum qui locutionem tuam
  corrigant.*
AHT-kway may-MAYN-toh, NOO-lee AHD-soont Roh-mah-
  NOH-ruhm KWEE loh-koo-tee-OH-nehm TOO-ahm KOH-ree-
  gahnt.

If a word has two syllables, put the stress on the first one. If it has
more than two, put the stress on the second-to-last syllable unless
both the second-to-last syllable and the last syllable are vowels.
When that happens, shift the stress back one syllable earlier.

So, for example, locutionem = "loh-koo-tee-OH-nehm," but lo-
cutio = "loh-KOO-tee-oh."

If the second-to-last syllable has an "i" in it and doesn't end in
a consonant, the stress is usually moved back one syllable. So, for
example, corrigant = "KOHR-ree-gahnt" and difficilius = "dee-
fee-KEE-lee-uss." For the same reason, the very common word ali-
qui (any) is pronounced "AH-lee-kwee."

ABOUT
THE AUTHOR
De Scriptore

HENRY BEARD spent a good part of his wonder years reading the works of Caesar, Cicero, Virgil, Horace, Catullus, and Plautus, never dreaming that his involuntary dedication to a dead language would put him in a perfect position, three decades later, to get in on the ground floor of the booming Latin market. He is the author of *Lingua Latina Occasionibus Omnibus* (Latin for All Occasions), the predecessor to this volume, and has also written a number of books in a live language, including *Sailing: A Sailor's Dictionary* and *Miss Piggy's Guide to Life*. When he is not hard at work alleviating the critical national Latin shortage, Mr. Beard pursues his studies of pet linguistics and plays golf, a pair of pastimes that will lead in due time to two forthcoming Villard titles: *French for Cats* and *The Official Exceptions to the Rules of Golf*.